achilles

by

Ayodele Ojomo

Copyright © Ojomo Ayodele Olaitan 2020
All rights reserved.

This book may not be reproduced, transmitted, or stored in whole or part in any retrieval system without written permission from the author except in the case of brief quotation embodied in critical articles and reviews.

These are all works of fiction. The events and characters described herein are imaginary and are not intended to refer to specific places or living persons. Any resemblance to real persons, living or dead is purely coincidental.

ACKNOWLEDGEMENT

To my creator, I am eternally grateful for life.
To my elder Sister Kemi, that believed in me when no one else did.
To Banke and Yinoluwa, our bond is forever, may blood never betray us.

TABLE OF CONTENTS

Acknowledgement 3

Table Of Contents 4

Preface 5

Aqua 7

Ignis 10

Caeli 13

Tellus 16

Profecti Confluentis 19

Dike 20

Ada 23

PREFACE

Have you ever been at a gathering of your family, distant relations and thought what if the overhead fan falls and lops off everyone's head, blood and organs splattered everywhere?

Have you ever been in a crowd and wondered what if an earthquake occurs and swallows everyone? Or a truck with failed breaks just rams into everyone and kills them.

Have you ever been to a party and felt so alone or out of place? Or being in class and daydreamed so deep that you were surviving a viral apocalypse with the love of your life. Or possessing superpowers, being a superhero, saving the world and dying in the process?

Do you have a problem of remembering too much of everything? Or forgetting nothing at all?

To be in the present, your mind just rewinds very fast backwards to a specific period in time when you experienced intense pain, embarrassment, loneliness or hurt and have those feelings wash over you again?

This is the kind of mind I possess, dark, horrific and deep but it is mine and I write this for those who share it with me and are struggling to come to terms with it.

It is a blessing and a curse.

But......

You Are Not Alone.

AQUA

You cannot fight the river
And want to fish from it
It will swallow you whole.

Water,
When it's cold its soothing
When it's hot it scalds the skin
So it is, with all things

If the earth decides to ban everyone of us,
Into space due to the manner we have been living on it
I would be in full support
Every last one of us

Only love knows all the atrocities that has been committed in its name
Only it bears the grief and pain
And only it revels in its joy

They do not always lose you
Admit it
You have lost people too
Consciously or unconsciously

Running water is nothing to a rock
But a surge of flood water, can move heavy boulders.
There's power in everything, *find it.*

Body bruised
Heart shattered
Spirit near death
In a raggedy voice I said "I need to heal"
Time looked at me and said *ready when you are*

If wickedness is evil,
And revenge is sin
If forgiveness is good,
Then my silence to you is death,
And death is a saint.

Nobody knows what nobody knows.
What you do not know, cannot kill you
But what you do know and pretend not to know,
Can come back to hunt you.
We drink the truth, spit it out
Then rinse our mouth with lies.
That is why our words are foul and reek of hate.

Be weary of the one who does not dig the mud pit as you do.
When he speaks,
Take his words with levity.
He can never know the depth of the well,
Pain has dug into you.

If you have a conscience,
taking repeatedly from a person without giving.
Physically and emotionally,
should make you feel guilty.
In a way.

Anything can last.
It depends on how well you choose to remember it
or let it go.

Words.....
They have birthed the greatest good.
The have spawned the greatest evil.
Use them wisely.
They are power.

IGNIS

Fire is only fire
You hate it when it burns.
You love it when it heats your food
Is that not the trait of hypocrites?

Vanity.
It's what you call it when you are poor
It's what you call it when you are struggling
The rich call it comfortability.

In this land, everybody walks around with an unbridled anger
Ready to spill out at the slightest provocation.
Some crack skulls while others crack hearts
But I bid you,
Do not walk around like the police
Those black jazz filled with vinegar, have no joy in their hearts or souls

Anger is evil
but when channeled rightly
is bliss to the very end.

Choose your addictions wisely
For in the end, they will define you.

The earth says "till me"
The woman says "till me"
The society says "give me"
Pressure is a noose tied around his neck
His name is called "Man"

Where I come from,
A boyfriend is supposed to be the deputy holy spirit
He is supposed to know his lady's mood swings.
And know the thoughts of her heart,
Even without her speaking her mind.
He is a poverty alleviation scheme.
God help us

No, not like a leech to your skin
Like a baby to a mother's bosom,
Attach yourself to any beneficial relationship
And give what you have to offer wholeheartedly.
But when it begins to get toxic like mud in a pool of water,
Detach yourself like a prey escapes its predator.
With haste, narrowly, on your heels,
With prayers to your God.

In this land,
The justice system is "no face no Case"
If you steal and get caught, you are on your own.
If you steal successfully, you are either made a chief, king or given a political position
But in all honesty,
Ole ni everybody

He who stands at the right is right
He who stands at the left is wrong
He who neither stands at the right nor at the left is not to be trusted.
He is not included in the affairs of men
He stands for himself
Neutrality is the worst of the worst
Nobody likes a two-faced person.

Only cowards and people who have something to hide do things secretly.
Make sure you do everything with your chest.
No man born of a woman will kill you.

I am not here to make you feel good.
I am not here to caress your ego.
I am here to tell you,
we are all broken and vulnerable and in need of help.
In different ways,
Some more than others.

CAELI

The end does not always justify the means.
What if you were the means,
To your own end

The earth does not hide it's soil.
Nor does the river stash it's water.
The sun does not horde it's light
Neither does the moon
If the breeze does not stifle it's air
Then who are you not to be selfless

You have a plate of jollof rice and assorted meat in front of you
Somebody has a pizza or a sharwama on their plate across your table
You look at their table and your mouth begins to water
So much so that you can kill for it.
That is envy and discontentment
And you are disrespecting our legendary jollof rice

The same wind that bends the bamboo,
Will snap a tree in half.
Know who you are.
Know your limits.
Pride will get you nowhere.

When a relationship ends and the other person has moved on
It is not for you to judge the strength of their love,
For what you both once had.
They have moved on.
Respect their healed process.
They have healed.
As should you

On Sundays, on a cool evening breeze.
Listening to people, preferring solutions to their problems with my little two cents
On other days, I am a tornado.
Fierce, angry, broken, lashing out and unable to take my own advice.
Destroying everything in my path.

And then my mind said
"If you do not give me to eat, whatever I see to eat,
And you will bear the consequences"

I see no difference between a master and a slave
Opportunity is a rift that separates the two.
Because if the roles were reversed,
The slave becomes something else.
If not worse than a master

When your deeds are purely elicited in favor of someone,
Know that disappointment and heartbreak,
are a stone throw away.

I like people who believe,
The light is not the only one that reveals things.
The darkness does as well………
It reveals the light in people.

The sun rises, you whine.
The moon emerges, you frown.
You say, I prefer the moon to the sun
or the sun to the moon.
Which in actual fact is untrue.
For no one would like it,
If the moon graces us with its light all night and all day.
Not even you.
They both do what they should, in the best way possible.
And should be appreciated in the same way.

TELLUS

You only appreciate the ground
When you fall,
and fall hard
Mother earth is always there, like a protective mother.
Ready to catch you

The difference between a bad thing and a good thing, is the person doing it
But what makes a good thing, good
Is the moment in which it is done.

It is in a noble man's character that he knows when to draw the line between
Obedience and oppression.
Reprimand and Anger.
Between blind selfishness and selflessness of those put under his care.

The worst thing you can do to a person
Is to allow them think back,
To the first time they laid their eyes on you.
and begin to shed tears.

We are all rich in some way.
We are all poor in some way.
For one to be said that "he is rich"
And for another to be said that "he is poor"

Both "poor" and "rich" are just mere words,
used to mask our deepest insecurities and pain.

Careful, with the praises you shower on me.
My imperfections might just spill out.
Then you will realize I am broken,
If not more than you.

You put your heart on your sleeves but it all gets blown to bits.
Time and time again.
Being bewitched by some voodoo powers would start to seem like a
logical explanation to your mind.
A drug which you feed your brain,
till you find out , you are not the only stowaway on the ship they call
Love.
Everyone carrying around pieces of themselves or none at all.
They are just better at hiding it.
And they tell you *"you have to as well, in order to survive"*.

A mango tree was planted and fruited successively for years.
All enjoyed of it's fruit .
But suddenly it stopped fruiting, its vigor drained, its branches were dry in its season
and the tree looked diseased.
They brutally cut it down without a second thought.
Forgetting all they have gained from it.
When it shielded them from the blazing sun with it's leaves.
How it served as a beautiful spot for their meeting with their lovers.
That is how most of you treat each other.
Without any second chances.

If you have to remind someone of the good you did him or her,
before they assist you in your time of need.
Best believe that individual, is not worthy of you.

If I tell you I'm surprised, believe me, I am truly.
But not at you, at me.
That I could be so totally seduced into your hands once more.
But far be it from me to complain.
Because I allowed it.

The blame rests on he who tries to change others.
But greater blame rests on he,
Who allows himself to be changed.

PROFECTI CONFLUENTIS

"Nature is one of the greatest teachers, sometimes we just need to be observant, quiet, listen and learn."

It was not the strokes of the cane that made Kate's eyes seep out hot tears, it was the fact that who she served the punishment for was also with the crowd, laughing. So here she was, under an apple tree licking her emotional wounds with a chicken and her two chicks sauntering around.

At that same instant, an eagle swooped in and poached one of the chicks, the chicken got hysterical, tried to fight off the eagle but there was little or nothing she could do. She could not fly after the eagle.

All these Kate watched intently under the tree, not that she could not help but she had enough pain as it was taking in twenty four strokes of cane for a measly love letter. The chicken kept cackling for some minutes, in the end, I guess she resigned to her fate and moved along with the remaining chick. "Maybe nature was teaching her a lesson" Kate wondered.

Sometimes life happens to us and there's nothing we can do about it. It will be painful, it will hurt, we might be broken but in the end we have to summon up the courage and move on just like the chicken did.

DIKE

I stopped believing in God when my father's throat was opened right before my eyes with a cutlass that could decapitate a buffalo's head in one swipe. We were covered in mud and scars, my mucus was pouring into my mouth, I wailed on. Nne strapped me to her back and sprinted like a cheetah. I have never in my life seen a woman move like that. "Kpaow!" I heard something go off, it was a gun, I thought this was the end, it whizzed past me and took off Nne's ear. Time did it's magic, fourteen years took me by surprise, I walk to and fro school on black tar, my headphones on. I was still trying to adjust to London. on our arrival my mum, she says dad had some connections before he left. That was the last time I visited the topic.

I opened the door and the smell of jollof rice wafted through all my senses. The only thing shackling my memories to my home.

I said in a low but audible voice "Nne ndewo".

She would always answer with a long hug and say "oo dim oma" even though I was not her husband and I will stroke her lost ear and tell her "imaranma".

Then in the evenings, there came that knock, there was always that annoying knock. Donald the P.I was always at my mum's heels like an unsolved murder case. He had a thick wavy hair that curled like that of the comic superhero Tony Stark which made him mildly attractive.

They would chat downstairs, their laughter reverberating through the whole house, I would grit and grind my teeth till my cheek muscles ached.

He would always come up to my room and try to initiate small talks but I would shut it down before it even began. As per man to man, I did not want him anywhere near Nne or I, I know how all this goes, first, it would be a hand extending a shake, then a hand extending gifts, before all is said and done, it will be a hand with all fingers flexed out on my Nne's face and a hand balled into a fist on mine. Moreover, the percentage of step parents that got along with their step children was not in any way encouraging, yes I did my homework and I was a nerd. A damn good one at that.

If Donald thought this house was a cave of treasures where he would recite the words "Open Sesame" and I would come welcome him with open arms, he was so wrong and he has my pity because he would grow old at the mouth of the cave.

Prom was here and Nne had gotten me an oversized suit, something that could contain two huge matured polar bears. I had to go from store to store searching for a well suited one. Two blocks from my school, there had just been a shootout, I don't know but my first reaction to those kind of scenes were just to walk past or run, but for some reason I felt drawn to the incident.

I noticed the car, it was the same as Donald's. I prayed it was not him but it was, he was riddled with bullets and bleeding profusely from a bullet hole in his neck. I held him in my arms, for that split moment I felt overwhelming guilt and pain crippling my heart into dust. I did not know when water began to run down my cheeks and I whispered "Nna m oo" under my breath. In his passenger's seat, placed comfortably was a sleek brand new suit with a note splattered with blood "For Dike".

It's when we are at our end, we accept the things we normally would not accept if the tides were calm. Sometimes pain and suffering can imprison us in their cavest and make us blind to love, true love. I know they say, "to err is human and to forgive is divine," but I forgot we breathe the same air, all of us, each and every one of us deserves new air.

ADA

Ada clambered to the doorstep with her baggage. Sweat was dripping from all corners of her rbody, which made her inner wear sticky, soaking her vintage blouse, it gripped tightly to her skin. The sun had no mercy, not today.

Reaching under the big flower vase, she extracted a key and let herself in. The flowery smell of the house welcomed her as she inhaled the scent, the parlor was a bit disorganized as usual, toys and books sprawled all over the place, her siblings might be stubborn, rebels to the bone but they knew when to draw the line when the matter concerned her.

She changed into her house clothes and began her chores.

School might have a vacation but that word does not exist in an African home and she was the first born. Besides she was saving herself all the trouble of doing them at night. As she washed the dishes, her mind flashed to the previous night in Tunde's AC room, a medical undergraduate, how he kept thrusting into her heavily while she just laid under him like a log of wood doing nothing, she literally had to fake an orgasm not to hurt his ego and this was not the first time this happened to her. To be frank, Tunde had no fault, his foreplay was excellent, he had a good mastery of the human body but she found sex with the opposite sex uninteresting and disgusting. The day she found Sandra's ass really enticing in the middle of Zoology lecture was the day she knew there was a problem.

The dishes were done, the parlor swept clean, everything arranged neatly, she felt she deserved a cold drink and headed for the fridge.

"Hun?! What's this?" She looked at a sticker note on the fridge.

It read "Ada, please there is corn in the kitchen cabinet and Ube in the fridge, you know what to do with them. Be back from church soon. Love mom"

"Urrrgghhh!! Why?! Why o Why?!!" she groaned.

She knew the implication of that note and this was one of the major reasons she dreaded coming back home for any break.

She brought out the corns, peeled the husk, went to the backyard, got the charcoal pot, poured a sizeable amount of coal into the pot, added a little kerosene then struck a match. When the fire died out, she used a fan to feed it air until the coal were red. Then she put a wire gauze netted together on the coal, arranged the corn on it and put the ube beside the firs to heat it up. This food was to be prepared outdoors.

As she sat there on a small wooden stool, roasting corns, making sure that they were not burnt, her mind drifted back to Sandra, a flashback, before her departure from school. They were in her room, she had just shared an intimate hug with her, wishing her safe journey back home and yet she felt sparks flying all over her body, she wanted to rip her dress to shreds and run her lips all over her body. She did not even know if Sandra felt the same way because Sandra did not have a boyfriend either but Ada was being careful because this was treacherous waters and she did not want to admit her feelings to her then get shunned or shutdown. She would not be able to handle the mental and emotional pain. For all she knew Sandra might definitely conclude she was possessed or tell her to the authorities. She would end up bagging some serious jail term. Why was life so hard?

The sparks that flew out from the fire jolted her to reality as they touched her legs.

"Ewooo!!" she wailed as she jumped away from the flames, she checked the perfectly roasted corns, took them out and replaced them with raw ones simultaneously for the Ubes as well, they just needed little heat, if the heat was much, they would dry up and burn.

Ada looked up to the moon and wondered what kind of life this was,

"Pon!Pon!Pon!" A car horn sounded at the gate, they were back. Ada scrambled to her feet and raced to the gate. In her mind, questions pounded with every heartbeat.

How would she explain to her staunch Catholic father and mother coupled with her siblings that she liked girls

How??? In what world was that possible?!!

She would rather take this secret to her grave.

Why? because this is Nigeria and people have been killed for less.

Far less.

They call me "an old soul in a young body"
But even old souls, need young voices,
Chirping about to make it laugh.
Not just being buried,
by the sound of the hollow reverberation echo,
its walls make when struck by beats of intense emotions.

Our senses do not bow to our commands.
They act of their own volition.
Noticing things we want to forget.
Feeling when we prefer to be as frigid as ice.
We would wonder why some human beings never cry or laugh.
Some might just drop dead like worn out slaves.
Thank God he did not put everything under our thumb.

A prayer is for when it is rocky
and for when there is pasture.
It is not for the things you can see and hear.
It is for when your back is turned.
The plans hatched under the cover of darkness, in your absence.
The word of mouth spread around against your name.
It is for those silent battles, you do not know
about and do not have the power to fight,
being fought on your behalf.
It is for those who believe.
Pray.....

My grandfather once said.....
Human beings are no different from chameleons.
When faced with immense pressure, danger
they change everything else but their skin.
In order to survive.

It is not that they do not love you.
The painful part is,
Realizing they do love you because of what you can do.
Now what will you do?

Things we need to learn, unlearn and relearn:
- ❖ People have a right to believe in what they believe.
- ❖ That your belief is different from mine, does not mean I should hate you.
- ❖ You cannot force a love, friendship or vibe, all things come from within.
- ❖ You can correct a person with love, devoid of insults and ridicule.
- ❖ Respect they say is reciprocal, the same way an adult is respected, a child should be as well.
- ❖ We all grew up in separate backgrounds with different norms and values as a framework of the society. Learn to accept it that some of those habits and norms you grew up with were wrong and change from them.
- ❖ Times change. So do we have to as well.
- ❖ Your acceptance signals growth.
- ❖ Do not lose long term relationships on the premise of a measly argument or disagreement. I can disagree with you on an issue and still be your friend.

Mama would always say "I want the best for you"
But when the worst happens,
She would say "maybe it's for the best"
I am left not knowing how to feel.

Perhaps one of the most heartbreaking and regrettable reminders
Of a scar
Is knowing it was all due to your actions.
Everyone comes with their greetings.
Empathies and sympathies wrapped in tiny little gift boxes except….
It's not your birthday.
It is the mourning of a great loss.
In the end
They will leave
And you will be left with your grief.

I am not trying to hide who I am.
From those I love.
But in the end, all it begets is hate.
Which is more pain than my heart can take.
So I try…
No more.

My mind is warped but I am thinking straight
And that is how all things end.
With you at the end of the blade or at its hilt.
The living hate you.
The dead loathe you.
Where do you belong?
Heaven is too pure for you.
Hell cannot harbor evil of your kind.
Where is your safe haven?
Where nothing lives or grows.
Is that how your heart is?

Printed in Great Britain
by Amazon